To my sweet Elanor,
for your love of
"cat - cat" ♡

Love, Grandma
Aug 2023

City the Kitty

by Lori Shepler

Foreword by Dr. Jennifer Conrad

City the Kitty Books

DEDICATION

This book is dedicated to the declawed cats of the world who have suffered so much and deserve so much better, and to the human beings who fight so hard to protect them from this inhumane and unnecessary procedure.

The True Leader in Orange.

It says in the ancient cat scripture that the new prophet will arrive at an hour when most of us are trying to sleep. It says he will rock the foundation when he lands. It says the new prophet will be an expert in his field, being blessed, wearing boxing gloves that are so soft, his hit brings enlightenment not harm.

He will fight against those who choose cruelty to make their profit. It says that he will be willful and adamant, yet gentle and caring. It says he will be short in stature but grand in presence. It says that he will be tireless, sleeping sometimes only 20 hours a day.

The future is being redirected because of him. History will be forever better because of him. He has seen the injustice of declawing and has an expertise he's graciously sharing with us. No one knows toes better.

He is a modern hero. Who hasn't heard of New York City? Kansas City? Mexico City? They all take their names from the grandest of beings, our orange tabby polydactyl Manx prophet, City the Kitty.

Jennifer Conrad, DVM
Founder and Director
The Paw Project

INTRODUCTION

I Had Her at Meow.

It's not often in a cat's life you show up on the right doorstep and it changes the course of your life in an instant.

Well this is a true story of how that really happened.

In one of those movie script beginnings, I somehow found my way to her. The right time, the right place, and the right person.

Destiny, meant to be, fate, or whatever words you want to use.

I found her in more ways than one.

I was an orange bedraggled ball of fun performing my antics in the gutter on a warm summer day in 2009. My nose and ears were stuffed with dirt. My usual white paws, faded to grey from my travels on the streets, dodging cars, fighting off predators, and trying to scavenge up my next meal.

I meowed and meowed and meowed and haven't stopped since.

My life in the first six months will remain a mystery because after all, that's what us cats are all about.

Let's just put it this way, I was looking for a place to la▮ I knew there was more than this tough but adventur▮ life I was leading. I wanted a safe roof over my he▮ the familiar sound of a can being opened with th▮ delectable treats in them, and someone to love wh▮ was in the mood.

I know it sounds crazy coming from a cat but I wan▮ to make more out of my 9 lives.

So there she was. She too was trying to find her ▮ and going through a rough patch since she had ▮ been laid off at her job at a major newspaper where ▮ had been a photojournalist for 25 years.

She was ready for a new purpose in life, was happ▮ be away from the doom and gloom of the strugg▮ newspaper business, and excited about the prosp▮ of painting a new Plan B canvas.

She needed me and I needed her.

She started doing what she does best and took lots lots of photos of me. I charmed her with my silliness charisma. I know I'm only a little cat but my person▮ stood out like a giant. She saw that I was ready illing to take on the world with my nub of a tail and aws the size of a lion.

y majestic and awesome claws lead the way.

the early days my curiosity pulled me to danger. oved chasing lizards into the streets, climbing as high I could up trees, exploring unfamiliar territories like e back of plumber's trucks only to escape as they ere about to drive off.

hen it was apparent that I had used up 8 of my 9 lives, days of wandering outside footloose and fancy e ended. Other than the occasional walk on a leash tside, I was destined to be an indoor kitty.

rough my funny and unique photos and videos, tarted amassing lots of interested fans. It was fulfilling know that we were bringing joy to people's lives.

t I wanted to help my fellow kitties even more mehow.

A declawed internet cat named Cassy told me about The Paw Project, a non-profit organization started in 2000 by Dr. Jennifer Conrad, to end declawing. I knew that I had found the path that I knew was out there, and that was to help end this inhumane procedure and make sure that all my fellow kitties will be safe from it someday. I made sure that my mom and I dedicate as much as we possibly can to this important cat cause.

This journey may have started in the gutter on that warm summer day, but we now know our purpose and where we are going.

City the Kitty

meow!
my name is City

I'm lucky because my doctor
went to veterinary school to
protect and save animals,
not to protect and save couches.

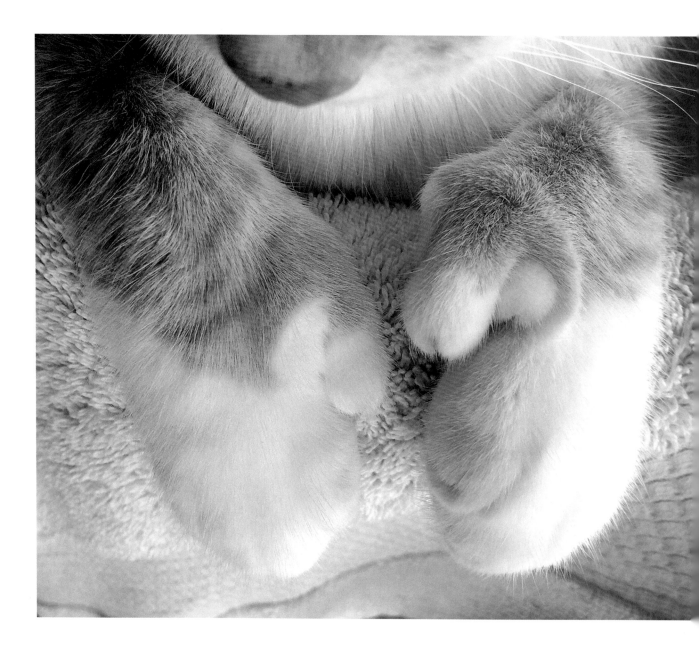

Two thumbs make a right.

Better get my sleep in now
before the kids get here.

Claws are part of what makes me so HANDsome.

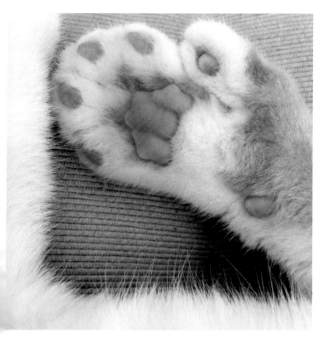

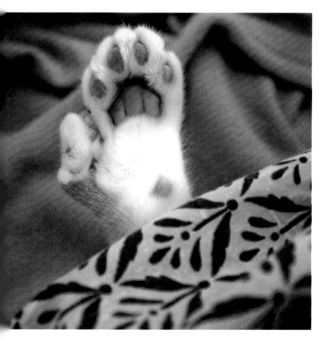

Is the vacuum gone yet?

Reading

makes

you

taller

and

smarter.

You

have

to

do

your

research

to

be

a spokescat.

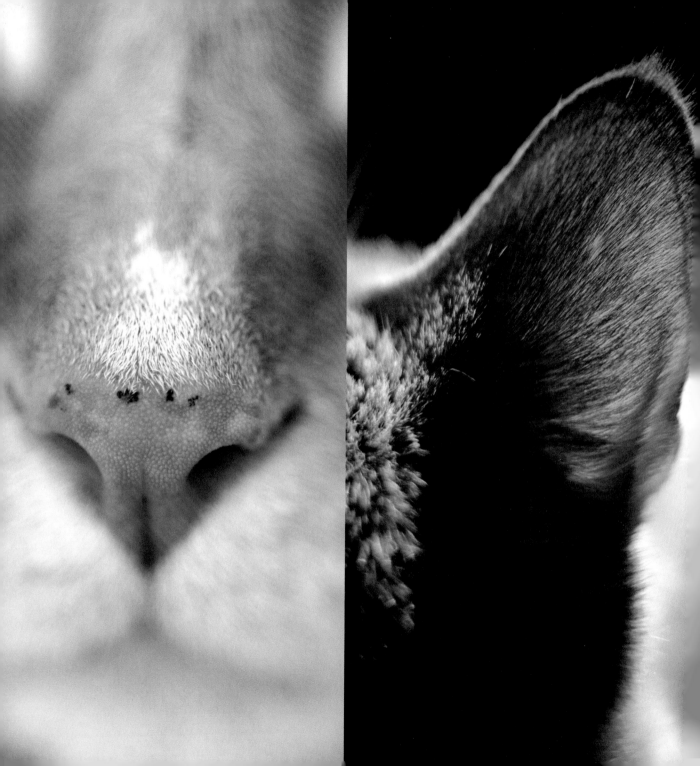

A wrong is never right.

It's a bird, it's a plane, it's City!

Leap for the stars.

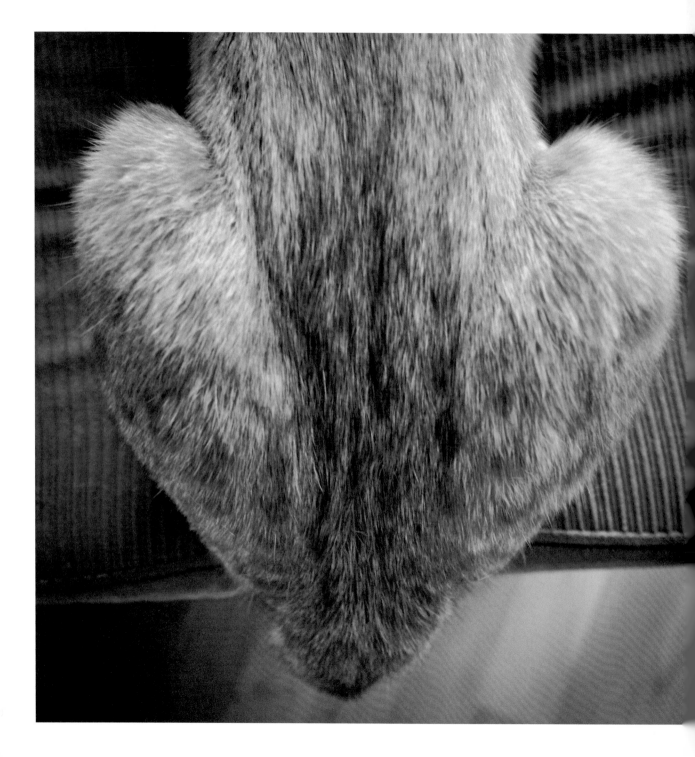

I love you this much.

Follow your special path.

Leave your mark in the world.

Be courteous and safe

Lend a paw or a hand when you can.

Nothing like a little bonding time.

Life

imitates

art.

Painting by Cheryl McCarley

tastrophicCreations.com

fectpost.com

DeziRoo.com

People really don't know how good it feels to scratch.
If they did, they would never declaw their cats.

The cat is out of the bag.

Never assume anything.

Never lose hope, tomorrow is a new day.

Never give up and always have faith.

Use your voice to help the voiceless.

The Doctor is in.

The Doctor is out.

Don't

Hide.

Stand

up

for

what

you

believe

in.

Healthy paws make healthy lives,
and healthy lives mean happy cats,
and happy cats mean happy owners.

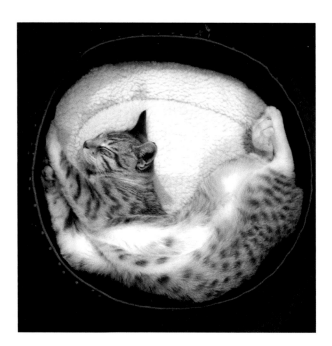

Time for a catnap.

Dream

Big.

ACKNOWLEDGMENTS

Many thanks to all our Kickstarter backers for your generous support. City the Kitty's first book would not have been possible without you.

Special thanks to Connie's Kittens, Jen Kondracki, Vegas Kitty, Lydia Swangren & Gracie Graylegs, and Pamela Ruth Weinman & Francis Stein.

Very special thanks to

 and

Dr. Marcy Hammerle
DVM DABVP,
The Pet Doctor

Nova

Thank you Howard Shen, the creative designer, for all the countless redesigns and awesome work that you do.

Thank you to Mel Melcon, Phuong Cotey Nguyen, Mick Rydlowski of Oskar & Klaus, Susan King and Atticus, Donna Drury, Cassandra Cat Drury, Kim Bressler, Dr. Jan Bahr, DeziRoo.com, Shanna Gilfix and Gabrielle Ruis, for your creative input and work.

Thanks to all the whistleblowers and people who work quietly behind the scenes to help end declawing. You are truly making a hugely positive difference for this important cause.

Thank you to all the veterinarians and veterinary professionals who are courageous enough to fight for cats and their wellbeing and who stand up against the status quo. Just because something has always been done doesn't mean it's right. Together, we will end declawing.

A heartfelt thank you to Dr. Jennifer Conrad and all the other ethical and humane veterinarians and people with the Paw Project, for your tireless, dedicated, and passionate work to save cats from being declawed. You all are true advocates for animals and think of the animals' needs first.

Thank you to my wife, Terra, for your unwavering support for all my cat projects and my work on this important cause to end declawing, even though you are a dog person. Thank you for what you do to help care for and save lives in your career as a Neuro-trauma ICU nurse.

Lori & City

ABOUT THE AUTHOR

For over 25 years, Lori Shepler captured moments of grace, passion, and excitement for readers as a prize-winning photographer with the Los Angeles Times.

Lori has a unique insight to the visual world.

Her pictures speak volumes. With three team Pulitzer Prizes won with her colleagues at the L.A. Times for their work on the Los Angeles Riots, The San Diego fires and the 1989 San Francisco earthquake, her work has earned the highest degree of professional validation three times over. Over the years at the LA Times she photographed countless celebrities, sporting events, concerts and breaking news. She now is a freelance photographer, City the Kitty's mom, and an author of two books, Pau Gasol, Life Vida with Kobe Bryant, and City the Kitty's first photo book.

I am City the Kitty,

I am the enemy of evil. I am the ally of all cats.

I am the enemy of evil because I protect kitties' toes.

I am the protector of paws.

I believe in my cause.

I am the enemy of injustice because I am a cat, and cats know right and wrong.

I am the ally of the underdog and anyone who cares to know me
  will know that I am fighting on the right side.

I believe good will prevail over bad.

I believe that David will prevail over Goliath: wrong, no matter how strong,
  is never right.

I believe that love is more powerful than hate.

I know you catch more with soft words than with brutal measures.

I believe veterinarians should honor their oath and heal, never inflicting
  unnecessary pain and suffering.

I believe that declawed cats are victims.

I believe all those who share their lives with cats should put the welfare of
  their kitties over the welfare of their possessions.

I believe doing anything and everything you can do to stop cruelty, pain, and
  suffering is more important than garnering money or keeping a piece of
  furniture pristine.

I am the enemy of apathy because I believe in effort.

No conscious being is born without valuing its life.

I am the enemy of the banality of evil because I am shining a spotlight on
  the cruelty and hypocrisy of declawing.

I am the voice for those who don't have one.

I am the enemy of evil.

Whose side are you on?

Paws Need Claws

All photography by Lori Shepler.
Cover and book design by Howard Shen.
Printed in the United States of America. First Printing, 2016
ISBN 978-0-615-79036-7   For more information, please visit www.citythekitty.com